meet *Emilie Richards*

Photo by Creation Waits

Now a USA TODAY bestselling author of women's fiction, Emilie Richards recalls fondly the months she served as a VISTA volunteer in the Arkansas Ozarks.

"This was the country's third poorest county," Emilie said in an interview from her Virginia home. "They had no phones, no safe water supply and no indoor plumbing. But the women created beauty out of nothing – turning scraps of old clothing and feedsacks into exquisitely beautiful quilts."

Emilie said the women insisted she quilt with them in the evenings, "and then later, they'd take out my stitches," she laughingly recalls of her early attempts at the craft.

The 20-year-old college student was left with a richness of experience and a love of quilting that would forever change her life and ultimately inspire a series of novels about the age-old craft. Emilie went on to finish her undergraduate degree in American studies and her master's in family development. She served as a therapist in a mental health center, as a parent services coordinator for Head Start families

[ ]d in several pastoral counseling centers. Now a full-time writer, Emilie has drawn on these experiences [whi]le crafting more than 50 novels.

[I]n *Wedding Ring*, the first Shenandoah Album novel, Emilie uses the stages of quilting as a metaphor [for] the cycles of marriage. In *Endless Chain*, Emilie's July 2005 hardcover novel, quilting serves as an [act]ivity that binds a community together in two parallel stories about human rights. Two pattern books, [*Qu*]*ilt Along with Emilie Richards* — *Wedding Ring* and *Endless Chain*, offer Emilie's fans a chance to [cre]ate their own versions of the quilts in her novels.

[A]nd Emilie has just been named the first member of ABC Quilts' National Advisory Board. The [no]n-profit group, headquartered in Northwood, N.H., teaches people of all ages to quilt and works to [pre]vent HIV/AIDS and alcohol and drug abuse. The group's international network of volunteers has [del]ivered over a half million quilts since they were founded in 1988.

[T]o learn more about Emilie Richards and ABC Quilts, visit Emilie's Web site at www.emilierichards.com.

LEISURE ARTS, INC.
Little Rock, Arkansas

read the books that *Inspired* the projects

Leisure Arts is pleased to offer these two quilting instruction books as companions to Emilie's compelling stories.

Quilt Along with Emilie Richards: Wedding Ring includes complete instructions for creating eight quilts from the story ... Wedding Ring, Friendship Album, North Carolina Lily, Tree of Life, Cissy's Pinwheel, Helen's Star, Simple Pleasures, and Sunbonnet Sue.

And if you would like to make Elisa's throw-sized Endless Chain Quilt, then you won't want to miss the second instruction book, *Quilt Along with Emilie Richards: Endless Chain*. This collection of six quilt patterns also includes Chinese Coins, Autumn Leaves, La Casa Amarilla, Clay's Choice, and Patriotic Sampler.

Enhanced with excerpts from the novels, each quilting instruction book gives the reader a glimpse of the compelling characters created by the gifted author.

The first two novels in Emilie Richards' **Shenandoah Album** series, *Wedding Ring* and *Endless Chain*, are rich with family drama, romance — and quilts!

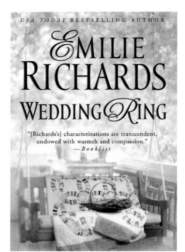
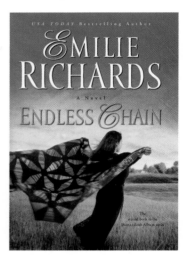

Read Emilie Richards' **Shenandoah Album** novels, then quilt along with the women of Toms Brook and Fitch Crossing Road. You may just discover a lifelong passion of your very own!

Endless Chain

sam kinkade

Sam Kinkade is finally feeling at home as a minister in rural Toms Brook, Virginia, reasonably content with his life and the Shenandoah Valley congregation. But his plans to welcome the area's growing Hispanic community to the church are suddenly met with resistance. Fortunately, when La Casa Amarilla, the church-run community center, is threatened, a stranger named Elisa Martinez walks through his door and Sam realizes he has found a woman capable of building bridges.

Elisa is an enigma. Although she slowly becomes involved in the community center, Sam is certain from her guarded manner that she is hiding something. Yet despite their growing friendship, Elisa won't discuss her past. Sam is intrigued with this Latina stranger, a woman who, despite the differences in their backgrounds, makes him only too aware of the intimacy missing in his life.

"Sam's wonderful at what he does, although not everyone thinks so. He's definitely controversial. I wonder sometimes if he's really happy here. He goes home every night to an empty house, and I think he's a man with a lot of love to give."

— Tessa MacCrae, Endless Chain

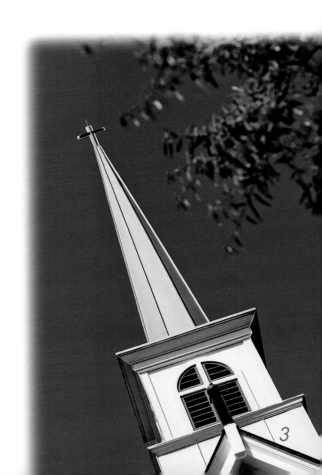

"Quilts mean so many different things to different people. But in the end, the quilts we make are always about something in our hearts."

— Tessa MacCrae, Endless Chain

"Elisa was addicted. She'd seen people addicted to the needle, but not to a quilting needle, a size 10 'between,' to be exact. Hand quilting was as mesmerizing as the click and whir of the antique treadle. Elisa had quickly found she could lose herself in the rivers of thread."

—from Endless Chain

elisa martinez

Elisa isn't looking to make friends let alone put down roots. She has come to hide. But despite her fears of discovery, she is enchanted by the beautiful work of and the friendship offered by the church women who invite her to join their quilting circle. And even though she fears the consequences for both of them, she finds herself powerfully drawn to Sam.

As she waits and prays for a reunion that may set her free, Elisa is captivated by a generations-old love story. Will she and Sam repeat the past, or can they find the love and the freedom they seek at last?

helen henry

When Elisa needs a place to stay, Helen is reluctant to open her home to the secretive young stranger. Helen is a fiercely private woman whose gruff exterior has protected her from a long life of loss and hardship. But as the days go by, the elderly woman discovers that Elisa shares her own love of quilts. As Elisa learns to piece her first quilt and joins the quilting bee at Helen's church, both women learn that the threads of friendship can weave themselves into the very fabric of a community, changing everyone in ways they could never have predicted.

"One look at Helen's expression and Elisa dismissed the possibility that she would be moving in with her. She could see that the family had made too much out of hiring a companion and completely antagonized the old woman in the process."
—from Endless Chain

With the warmth and comfort of a handmade quilt, *Endless Chain*— an exploration of the intricate patterns of family and community, and the threads that bind them together—will envelop and welcome readers into the richness of life in the Shenandoah Valley.

Endless Chain

Striped fabrics glow against a black background on Elisa's quilt. As she sewed the pieces, she found herself caught up in the rhythm of the quilt's creation. Learning to quilt provided a much-needed rest for the heroine of Endless Chain, a woman whose world was turned upside down and whose heart yearned for a life of peace, love, and contentment.

Finished Lap Quilt Size: 45" x 52" (114 cm x 132 cm)
Finished Block Size: 11" x 12³/₄" (28 cm x 32 cm)

lisa took the magazine and examined the photograph of a quilt. 'Endless Chain.' The ...ks *were hexagonal, with spokes radiating from a circle in the middle. The spokes connected,* ...hat *the design seemed to have no beginning and no end. Elisa said, 'It's like the fabrics are* ...ing hands.'"

—from Endless Chain

...TTING OUT THE PIECES

...ow **Template Cutting**, page 49, to cut fabric ...m templates. Patterns are on pages 10 – 11.

...**m black solid fabric:**
- Cut 116 **A's**.
- Cut 8 **B's**.
- Cut 18 **C's** for appliqués.
- Cut 4 **D's** for appliqués.

...**m assorted stripe fabrics:**
- Cut 120 **E's**.

YARDAGE REQUIREMENTS
Yardage is based on 43"/44" (109 cm/112 cm) wide fabric.

2³/₄ yds (2.5 m) of black solid fabric

1⁷/₈ yds (1.7 m) **total** of assorted stripe fabrics

3³/₈ yds (3.1 m) of backing fabric

⁷/₈ yd (80 cm) of binding fabric

You will also need: 53" x 60" (135 cm x 152 cm) rectangle of batting

7

Unit 1
(make 18)

Block
(make 18)

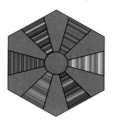

Unit 2
(make 4)

Half Block
(make 4)

Fig. 1

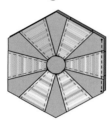

Row 1
(make 3)

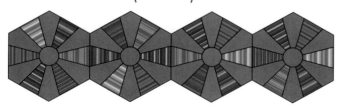

Row 2
(make 2)

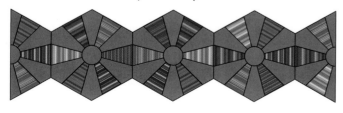

MAKING THE BLOCKS

*Follow **Piecing and Pressing**, page 49, and **Needle-turn Appliqué**, page 51, to make blocks.*

1. Matching dots, sew 6 **A's** and 6 **E's** together to make **Unit 1**. Stay stitch around center hole $1/8$" from raw edges. Make 18 **Unit 1's**.

2. Center 1 **C** over hole in 1 **Unit 1** and appliqué in place to complete **Block**. Make 18 **Blocks**.

3. Matching dots, sew 2 **A's**, 2 **B's**, and 3 **E's** together to make **Unit 2**. Stay stitch around center hole $1/8$" from raw edges. Make 4 **Unit 2's**.

4. Matching raw edges, center **D** over hole in 1 **Unit 2** and appliqué in place to complete **Half Block**. Make 4 **Half Blocks**.

ASSEMBLING THE QUILT TOP

1. To sew **Blocks** and **Half Blocks** together into **Rows**, refer to **Fig. 1** and sew from dot to dot, backstitching to reinforce at each dot. In this manner, sew 4 **Blocks** together to make **Row 1**. Make 3 **Row 1's**.

2. In the same manner, sew 2 **Half Blocks** and 3 **Blocks** together to make **Row 2**. Make 2 **Row 2's**.

3. To sew **Rows** together, sew each seam from dot to dot, backstitching at each dot and cutting thread before moving to next seam. Referring to **Quilt Assembly Diagram**, page 9, and alternating **Row 1's** and **Row 2's**, sew **Rows** together to complete quilt top.

...MPLETING THE QUILT

Follow **Quilting**, page 53, to mark, layer, and quilt as desired. Our quilt is machine quilted. Gold outline quilting is stitched in each striped piece, and "wavy" echo quilting fills the black pieced areas. The appliqués are not quilted.

Cut a 26" square of binding fabric. Follow **Binding**, page 60, to bind quilt using $2^1/2$"w bias binding with mitered corners.

Quilt Assembly Diagram

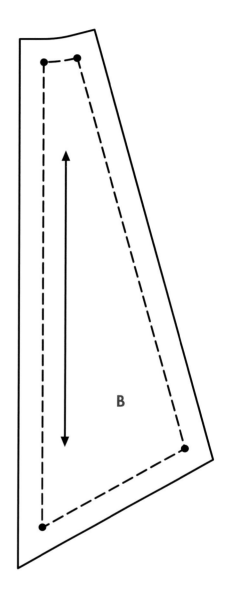

B

"*Elisa had never had a serious hobby, but piecing the endless chain quilt was a different story. Perhaps her interest had developed so quickly because piecing the quilt reminded her of fitting a puzzle together. Or perhaps it was the pursuit of beauty when her life had been so devoid of it. And perhaps it was the image the quilt created in her mind of links so strong they could never be broken.*"

—from Endless Chain

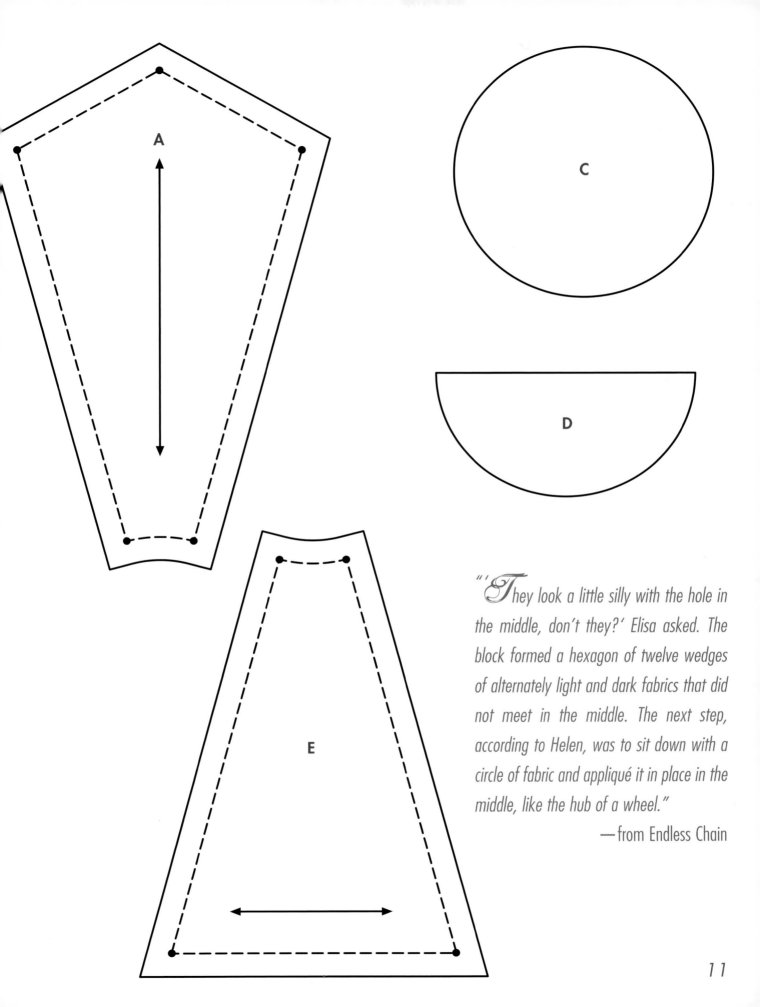

A

C

D

E

"'They look a little silly with the hole in the middle, don't they?' Elisa asked. The block formed a hexagon of twelve wedges of alternately light and dark fabrics that did not meet in the middle. The next step, according to Helen, was to sit down with a circle of fabric and appliqué it in place in the middle, like the hub of a wheel."

—from Endless Chain

When little Rory Brogan jumped in the middle of Cathy Adams' Chinese Coins quilt top, the horrified members of the quilting bee were surely glad to have access to Helen Henry's skill in repairing it. Helen didn't like children, but she had to admit that Rory had spunk ... although she would never say so out loud.

Finished Wall Hanging Size: 36" x 40" (91 cm x 102 cm)

CUTTING OUT THE PIECES

*Follow **Rotary Cutting**, page 48, to cut fabric. All strips are cut across the width of the fabric unless otherwise noted. All measurements include a $^1/_4$" seam allowance. Cutting lengths given for borders are exact.*

From black and gold print fabric:
- Cut 2 *lengthwise* **side outer borders** $5^1/_2$" x $39^1/_2$".
- Cut 2 *crosswise* **top/bottom outer borders** $5^1/_2$" x $25^1/_2$".

From black solid fabric:
- Cut 2 **side inner borders** $2^1/_4$" x $29^1/_2$".
- Cut 2 **top/bottom inner borders** $2^1/_4$" x 22".
- Cut 4 **sashing strips** $2^3/_4$" x 26".

From assorted print fabrics:
- Cut 1 or more 20"l **strips** from each fabric in widths varying from $1^1/_4$"w to $1^3/_4$"w.

"Cathy Adams brought a quilt top for show and tell in the Chinese Coin pattern, using oriental prints. We will begin quilting the top after Labor Day. Kate Brogan brought her two youngest children as guests. After Rory jumped on Cathy's quilt top, Chinese Coins will need all the help Helen can give it."

—Minutes from the Shenandoah Community Church Wednesday Morning Quilting Bee and Social Gathering, August 6, Endless Chain

YARDAGE REQUIREMENTS
Yardage is based on 43"/44" (109 cm/112 cm) wide fabric.

$1^1/_4$ yds (1.1 m) of black and gold print fabric

$^5/_8$ yd (57 cm) of black solid fabric

$1^1/_4$ yds (1.1 m) **total** of assorted print fabrics *(We used 16 different prints.)*

$1^1/_4$ yds (1.1 m) of backing fabric

$^3/_4$ yd (69 cm) of binding fabric

You will also need: 40" x 44" (102 cm x 112 cm) rectangle of batting

Strip Set

Unit 1
(make 5)

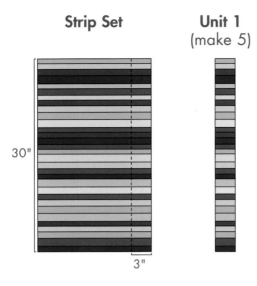

30"

3"

Wall Hanging Top Diagram

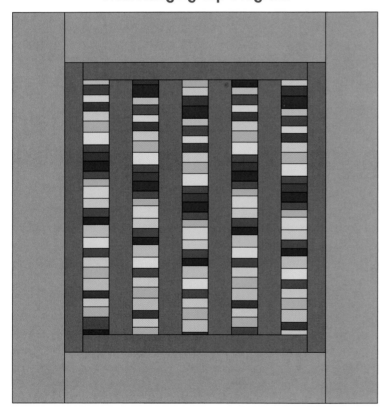

ASSEMBLING THE WALL HANGING T*

*Follow **Piecing and Pressing**, page 49, to make wall hanging top.*

1. Assemble **strips** randomly as shown to make a **Strip Set** 30"l. Cut across **Strip Set** at 3" intervals to make a tota of 5 **Unit 1's**.

2. To stagger the horizontal strips of **Unit 1** trim varying amounts from tops and bott to make each **Unit 1** measure 3" x 26".

3. Referring to **Wall Hanging Top Diagra** sew **Unit 1's** and **sashing strips** togethe to complete center section of wall hanging top. **(Note:** *If no directional prints were used, you may wish to rot some **Unit 1's** for more variety.)*

4. Matching centers and corners and eas in any fullness, sew **top**, **bottom**, and then **side inner borders** to center sectic of wall hanging top. In the same mann sew **outer borders** to wall hanging top

COMPLETING THE WALL HANGING

1. Follow **Quilting,** page 53, to mark, la and quilt as desired. Our wall hanging is machine quilted "in the ditch" arou the pieced strips and borders. A bamb pattern is quilted in the sashing strips. The outer borders have a combination of diagonal, vertical, and horizontal channel quilting.

2. Follow **Making a Hanging Sleeve**, page 59, if hanging sleeve is desired.

3. Cut a 22" square of binding fabric. Follow **Binding**, page 60, to bind wall hanging using $2^1/2$"w bias binding wi mitered corners.

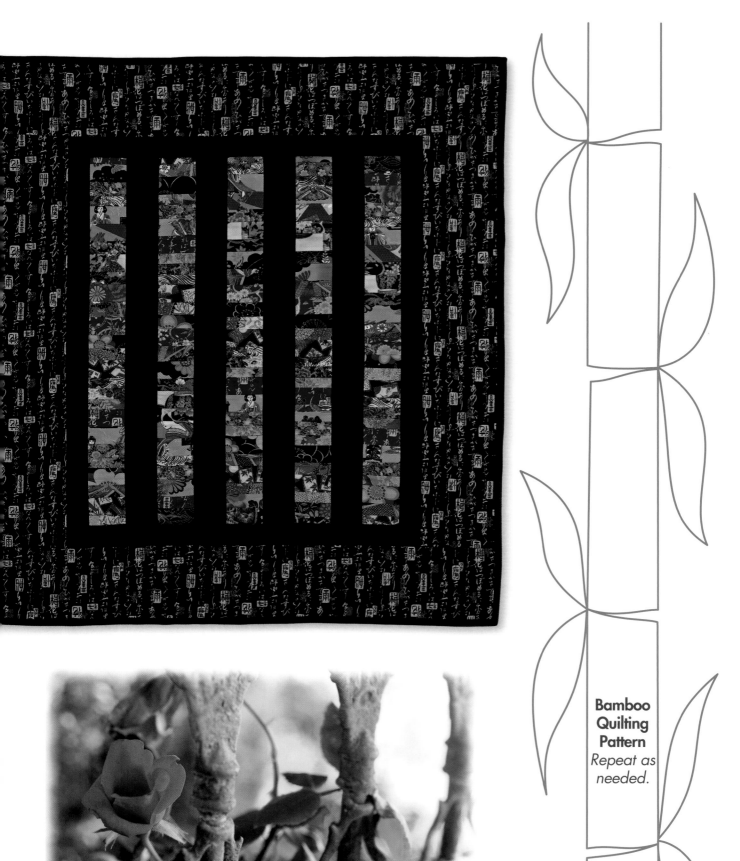

Bamboo Quilting Pattern
Repeat as needed.

Autumn Leaves

As the ladies of the Shenandoah Community Church Quilting Bee know, quilts are among the most personal gifts you can give. And a quilt of autumn leaves was an especially meaningful gift for Martha Wisner.

Quilt designed and made by Nan Slaughter.
Finished Lap Quilt Size: 57" x 73" (145 cm x 185 cm)
Finished Block Size: 8" x 8" (20 cm x 20 cm)

CUTTING OUT THE PIECES

*Follow **Rotary Cutting**, page 48, to cut fabric. All strips are cut across the width of the fabric unless otherwise noted. Borders include an extra 4" of length for "insurance" and will be trimmed after assembling quilt top center. All other measurements include a $1/4$" seam allowance. Refer to **Template Cutting**, page 49, to cut appliqué pieces. Appliqué pieces are on page 21 and do not include seam allowance.*

From assorted green print fabrics:
- Cut 288 **squares** $2^1/2$" x $2^1/2$".

From 2 cream print fabrics:
- Cut a **total** of 17 **background squares** $9^1/2$" x $9^1/2$".

From yellow, gold, brown, and red print fabrics:
- Cut 6 **each** of **leaves A** and **B** and 5 **leaves C** from patterns. *(Some leaves may be reversed, if desired.)*

From black and white mini-check fabric:
- Cut 1 strip $7^1/2$" wide. From this strip, cut 34 **small rectangles** 1" x $7^1/2$".
- Cut 1 strip $8^1/2$" wide. From this strip, cut 34 **large rectangles** 1" x $8^1/2$".

From green and orange stripe fabric:
- Cut 16 **borders strips** 1"w.

From black and white plaid border fabric:
- Cut 2 *lengthwise* **side fourth borders** 4" x $69^1/2$".
- Cut 2 *lengthwise* **top/bottom fourth borders** 4" x $60^1/2$".
- Cut 2 *lengthwise* **side second borders** 4" x $61^1/2$".
- Cut 2 *lengthwise* **top/bottom second borders** 4" x $52^1/2$".

YARDAGE REQUIREMENTS

Yardage is based on 43"/44" (109 cm/112 cm) wide fabric.

$1^3/8$ yds (1.3 m) **total** of assorted green print fabrics

$1^1/2$ yds (1.4 m) **total** of 2 cream print fabrics

Scraps of yellow, gold, brown, and red print fabrics

$1/2$ yd (46 cm) of black and white mini-check fabric

$1/2$ yd (46 cm) of green and orange stripe fabric

$2^1/8$ yds (1.9 m) of black and white plaid fabric

$4^1/2$ yds (4.1 m) of backing fabric

$7/8$ yd (80 cm) of binding fabric

You will also need: 65" x 81" (165 cm x 206 cm) rectangle of batting

Template plastic

Unit 1
(make 72)

Patchwork Block
(make 18)

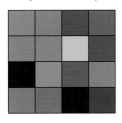

Unit 2
(make 17)

Leaf Block
(make 17)

MAKING THE BLOCKS

*Follow **Piecing** and **Pressing**, page 49, and **Needle-turn Appliqué**, page 51, to make blocks. Use a $^1/_4$" seam allowance for all seams.*

1. Sew 4 assorted green print **squares** together to make **Unit 1**. Make 72 **Unit 1's**.

2. Sew 4 **Unit 1's** together to make **Patchwork Block**. Make 18 **Patchwork Blocks**.

3. Center a **leaf** on 1 cream **background square** and appliqué in place. Making sure appliquéd leaf is centered, trim **background square** to $7^1/_2$" x $7^1/_2$" to make **Unit 2**. Make 17 **Unit 2's**.

4. Sew 1 **small rectangle** to each side, 1 **large rectangle** to the top, and 1 **large rectangle** to the bottom of **Unit 2** to make **Leaf Block**. Make 17 **Leaf Blocks**.

ASSEMBLING THE QUILT TOP CENTER

1. Beginning with a **Patchwork Block** and alternating blocks, sew 3 **Patchwork Blocks** and 2 **Leaf Blocks** together to make **Row 1**. Make 4 **Row 1's**.

2. Beginning with a **Leaf Block** and alternating blocks, sew 3 **Leaf Blocks** and 2 **Patchwork Blocks** together to make **Row 2**. Make 3 **Row 2's**.

3. Alternating rows, sew **Row 1's** and **Row 2's** together to complete quilt top center.

ADDING THE BORDERS

*Refer to **Quilt Top Diagram**, page 19, for placement.*

1. Sew 2 **border strips** together end to end to make 1 **border**. Make 4 **first borders** and 4 **third borders**.

2. To determine length of **side first borders**, measure *length* of quilt top center. Trim **side first borders** to determined length. Matching centers and corners, sew **side first borders** to quilt top.

3. To determine length of **top/bottom first borders**, measure *width* of quilt top center (including added borders). Trim **top/bottom first borders** to determined length. Matching centers and corners, sew **top/bottom first borders** to quilt top.

4. Repeat Steps 2 – 3 to sew **second**, **third**, and **fourth borders** to quilt top.

COMPLETING THE QUILT

1. Follow **Quilting**, page 53, to mark, layer, and quilt as desired. Our quilt was machine meander quilted over the entire quilt except for the appliqués and green and orange stripe borders.

2. Cut a 28" square of binding fabric. Follow **Binding**, page 60, to bind quilt using $2^1/_2$"w bias binding with mitered corners.

Quilt Top Diagram

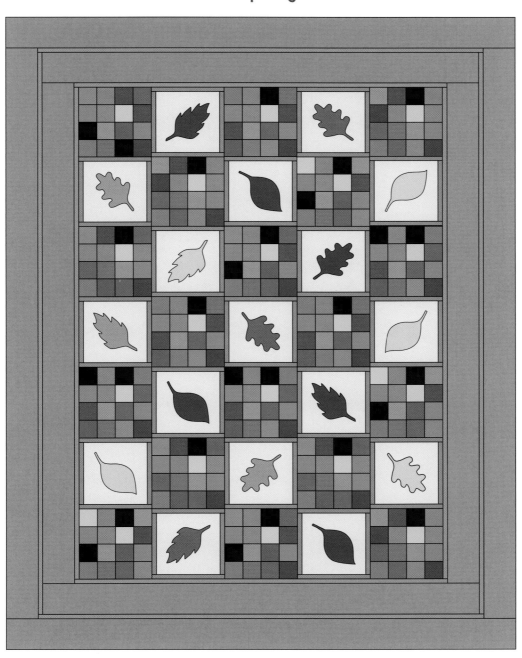

"*The lap quilt, with appliquéd leaves in autumn colors, was* be a gift for Martha Wisner, who had been the church secret for many years. She had moved into an assisted living facil several years before and was now in the nursing home wing. T quilters had chosen the pattern because Martha had loved fall their Shenandoah Valley."

—from Endless Ch

La Casa Amarilla

*H*appiness is the essence of this colorful little quilt! It's easy to imagine it brightening the walls of *La Casa Amarilla* (the yellow house), the fictional community center for the Spanish-speaking children of Shenandoah Valley. Because this quilt's joyful hues give it shape and motion, the pattern was kept simple. So whether you're a beginning quilter or you've quilted for years, you'll enjoy creating your own version of this rainbow-colored artwork.

Quilt designed and made by Bonnie Olaveson.
Finished Wall Hanging Size: 44" x 44" (112 cm x 112 cm)
Finished Block Size: 7" x 7" (18 cm x 18 cm)

CUTTING OUT THE PIECES

*Follow **Rotary Cutting**, page 48, to cut fabric. All strips are cut across the width of the fabric unless otherwise noted. Borders include an extra 4" of length for "insurance" and will be trimmed after assembling wall hanging top center. All other measurements include a ¹/₄" seam allowance. Refer to **Preparing Fusible Appliqué Pieces**, page 51, to cut appliqué pieces. Appliqué patterns are on page 27 and are reversed.*

From yellow print fabric:
- Cut 2 *lengthwise* **side outer borders** 2¹/₂" x 47¹/₂".
- Cut 2 *lengthwise* **top/bottom outer borders** 2¹/₂" x 43¹/₂".
- Cut 2 *lengthwise* **side inner borders** 1¹/₂" x 41¹/₂".
- Cut 2 *lengthwise* **top/bottom inner borders** 1¹/₂" x 39¹/₂".
  From remaining width:
- Cut 13 **stars** for appliqué.

From *each* of assorted print fabrics:
- Cut 3 **strips** 1¹/₂"w.
- Cut 1 **swirl** and **dot** for appliqué (cut a **total** of 13 **swirls** with **matching dots**).

"*We have taken it upon ourselves to make wall hangings and lap quilts for La Casa Amarilla, which will soon be filled with children each school day afternoon. Of course, in keeping with the theme, each quilt must have yellow in its pattern.*"

—*Minutes from the Shenandoah Community Church Wednesday Morning Quilting Bee and Social Gathering, August 6, Endless Chain*

YARDAGE REQUIREMENTS
Yardage is based on 43"/44" (109 cm/112 cm) wide fabric.

1¹/₂ yds (1.4 m) of yellow fabric

¹/₄ yd (23 cm) **each** of 14 assorted print fabrics

2³/₄ yds (2.5 m) of backing fabric

³/₄ yd (69 cm) of binding fabric

You will also need:
48" x 48" (122 cm x 122 cm) square of batting

Fusible web

Stabilizer

Strip Set A (make 3)

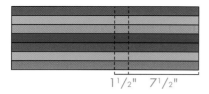

1½" 7½"

Block A   **Border Unit A**
(make 12)   (make 11)

Strip Set B (make 3)

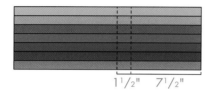

1½" 7½"

Unit 1   **Border Unit B**
(make 13)   (make 11)

Block B (make 13)

Row 1 (make 3)

Row 2 (make 2)

MAKING THE BLOCKS AND BORDER UNITS

*Follow **Piecing and Pressing**, page 49, and **Machine Decorative Stitch Appliqué**, page 52, to make blocks and border units.*

1. Sew 7 assorted **strips** together to make **Strip Set A**. Make 3 identical **Strip Set A's**. Cut across **Strip Set** at 7½" intervals to make 12 **Block A's**. Cut across remainders of **Strip Set A's** at 1½" intervals to mal 11 **Border Unit A's**.

2. Sew 7 assorted **strips** together to make **Strip Set B**. Make 3 identical **Strip Set B's**. Cut across **Strip Set** at 7½" intervals to make 13 **Unit 1's**. Cut across remainders of **Strip Set B's** at 1½" intervals to mal 11 **Border Unit B's**.

3. Referring to **Block B** diagram, appliqué 1 **star** and 1 **swirl** and matching **dot** to center of each **Unit 1** to make **Block B**. Make 13 **Block B's**.

ASSEMBLING THE WALL HANGING TOP CENTER

1. Sew 3 **Block B's** and 2 **Block A's** together to make **Row 1**. Make 3 **Row 1's**.

2. Sew 3 **Block A's** and 2 **Block B's** together to make **Row 2**. Make 3 **Row 2's**.

3. Sew **Rows** together to complete wall hanging top center.

ADDING THE BORDERS

*Refer to **Wall Hanging Top Diagram**, page 25, for placement.*

1. To determine length of **top/bottom inner borders**, measure *width* of wall hanging top center. Trim **top/bottom inner borders** to determined length. Matching centers and corners, sew **top/bottom inner borders** to wall hanging top.

2. To determine length of **side inner borders**, measur *length* of wall hanging top center (including adde borders). Trim **side inner borders** to determined length. Matching centers and corners, sew **side inner borders** to wall hanging top.

Alternating **Border Units**, sew 3 **Border Unit A's** and 3 **Border Unit B's** together end to end. Remove 5 squares from one end to make **top middle border**. Repeat to make **bottom middle border**.

Alternating **Border Units**, sew 3 **Border Unit A's** and 3 **Border Unit B's** together end to end. Remove 3 squares from one end to make **side middle border**. Make 2 **side middle borders**.

Matching centers and corners and easing in any fullness, sew **top**, **bottom**, and then **side middle borders** to wall hanging top.

Repeat Steps 1 – 2 to sew **outer borders** to wall hanging top.

COMPLETING THE WALL HANGING

Follow **Quilting,** page 53, to mark, layer, and quilt as desired. Our wall hanging is machine meander quilted.

Follow **Making a Hanging Sleeve**, page 59, if hanging sleeve is desired.

Cut a 23" square of binding fabric. Follow **Binding**, page 60, to bind wall hanging using 2^1/$_2$"w bias binding with mitered corners.

Wall Hanging Top Diagram

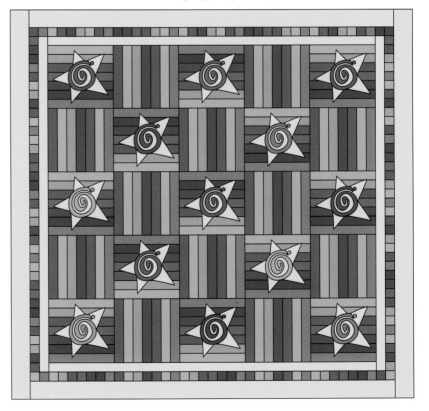

"*They were headed toward an old frame farmhouse painted lemon-yellow. It was set back from the church, at least an acre to the northwest. A narrow gravel drive snaked to the front porch from the road ... the house itself sat in a field of Queen Anne's lace and brilliant blue chicory, black-eyed Susans and puff-ball dandelions. The effect was charming.*

'La Casa Amarilla,' Elisa read. 'Good choice for a name. Very definitely a yellow house.'"

—from Endless Chain

Star

Dot

Swirl

Clay's Choice

In *Endless Chain*, the ladies of the Shenandoah Community Church Quilting Bee created a Clay's Choice quilt in Christmas colors to raffle at their church bazaar. But as you can see, the pattern is lovely in other colors. Helen Henry asked who the quilt pattern was named for, but no one in the quilting bee knew the answer. They would have been interested to know that Henry Clay was an American statesman in the early 1800's, and one of his many passions included fostering good relations with Latin America.

Finished Quilt Size: 91" x 106" (231 cm x 269 cm)
Finished Block Size: 8" x 8" (20 cm x 20 cm)

...TTING OUT THE PIECES

...ow *Rotary Cutting*, page 48, to cut fabric. All strips are cut across the width ...he fabric unless otherwise noted. Borders include an extra 4" of length for ...urance" and will be trimmed after assembling quilt top center. All other ...asurements include a $1/4$" seam allowance.

...m black print fabric:

- Cut 20 strips $2^7/8$"w. From these strips, cut 252 **large squares** $2^7/8$" x $2^7/8$".
- Cut 2 *lengthwise* **side outer borders** $3^1/2$" x $103^1/2$".
- Cut 2 *lengthwise* **top/bottom outer borders** $3^1/2$" x $94^1/2$".
- Cut 2 *lengthwise* **side inner borders** $3^1/2$" x $92^1/2$".
- Cut 2 *lengthwise* **top/bottom inner borders** 3" x $82^1/2$". **(Note: Top/bottom inner borders** are cut narrower than **side inner borders**.)

From remaining width:

- Cut 36 strips $2^7/8$"w. From these strips, cut 144 **large squares** $2^7/8$" x $2^7/8$".

...m cream solid fabric:

- Cut 16 strips $2^7/8$"w. From these strips, cut 198 **large squares** $2^7/8$" x $2^7/8$".
- Cut 25 strips $2^1/2$"w. From these strips, cut 396 **small squares** $2^1/2$" x $2^1/2$".
- Cut 7 strips $4^1/4$"w. From these strips, cut 59 squares $4^1/4$" x $4^1/4$". Cut squares **twice** diagonally to make 236 **border triangles**.

...m yellow print fabric:

- Cut 25 strips $2^1/2$"w. From these strips, cut 396 **small squares** $2^1/2$" x $2^1/2$".

...m *each* red print, blue print, and green print fabric:

- Cut 2 strips $2^5/8$"w. From these strips, cut 19 **or** 20 **border squares** $2^5/8$" x $2^5/8$" to make a **total** of 118 **border squares**.
- Cut 3 strips $2^7/8$"w. From these strips, cut 32 **large squares** $2^7/8$" x $2^7/8$" from 1 red, 1 blue, and 1 green print fabric, and 34 **large squares** from remaining strips for a **total** of 198 **large squares**.

YARDAGE REQUIREMENTS

Yardage is based on 43"/44" (109 cm/112 cm) wide fabric.

5 yds (4.6 m) of black print fabric

$4^1/4$ yds (3.9 m) of cream solid fabric

2 yds (1.8 m) of yellow print fabric

$1/2$ yd (46 cm) **each** of 2 red, 2 blue, and 2 green print fabrics

$8^1/4$ yds (7.5 m) of backing fabric

$1^1/8$ yds (1 m) of binding fabric

You will also need: 99" x 114" (251 cm x 290 cm) rectangle of batting

"*Are* you a quilter?" Helen asked Kendra Taylor.

"I collect old quilts," Kendra said. "I like the history and the stories that come with them. What pattern is this? A pinwheel of some sort, right?"

"Clay's Choice," Helen said. "Don't know why it's called that. Who was this Clay, anyway?"

—from Endless Chain

Fig. 1

Triangle-Square A's
(make 396)

Triangle-Square B's
(make a **total** of 396)

Unit 1
(make 396)

Unit 2
(make 99)

Unit 3
(make 99)

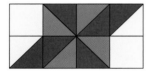

Unit 4
(make 198)

Block
(make 99)

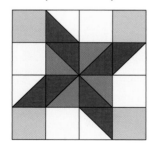

MAKING THE BLOCKS

*Follow **Piecing and Pressing**, page 49, to make blocks.*

1. Draw diagonal line (corner to corner) on wrong side of each cream **large square**. With right sides together, place 1 cream **large square** on top of 1 black **large square**. Stitch seam ¹/₄" from each side of drawn line (**Fig. 1**)

2. Cut along drawn line and press seam allowance to darker fabric to make 2 **Triangle-Square A's**. Make 396 **Triangle-Square A's**.

3. Repeat Steps 1 – 2 using red, blue, and green **large squares** and black **large squares** to make a total of 396 **Triangle-Square B's**. (You will need 1 set of 4 matching **Triangle-Square B's** for **each** of the 99 Blocks needed for the quilt.)

4. Sew 1 cream **small square** and 1 **Triangle-Square A** together to make **Unit 1**. Make 396 **Unit 1's**.

5. Sew 4 matching **Triangle-Square B's** together to make **Unit 2**. Make 99 **Unit 2's**.

6. Sew 2 **Unit 1's** and 1 **Unit 2** together to make **Unit 3**. Make 99 **Unit 3's**.

7. Sew 2 yellow **small squares** and 1 **Unit 1** together to make **Unit 4**. Make 198 **Unit 4's**.

8. Sew 2 **Unit 4's** and 1 **Unit 3** together to make **Block**. Make 99 **Blocks**.

ASSEMBLING THE QUILT TOP CENTER

1. Referring to **Quilt Assembly Diagram**, page 32, sew 9 **Blocks** together to make **Row**. Make 11 Rows.

2. Sew **Rows** together to make center section of quilt top.

~KING THE PIECED BORDERS

Sew 1 **border square** and 2 **border triangles** together to make **Border Unit**. Make 114 **Border Units**.

Sew 1 **border square** and 2 **border triangles** together to make **Corner Border Unit**. Make 4 **Corner Border Units**.

In random color order, sew 26 **Border Units** and 1 **Corner Border Unit** together to make **top/bottom pieced border**. Make 2 **top/bottom pieced borders**.

In random color order, sew 31 **Border Units** and 1 **Corner Border Unit** together to make **side pieced border**. Make 2 **Side Pieced Borders**.

~DING THE BORDERS

~r to **Quilt Assembly Diagram**, page 32, ~lacement.

To determine length of **side inner borders**, measure *length* of quilt top center. Trim **side inner borders** to determined length. Matching centers and corners, sew **side inner borders** to quilt top.

To determine length of **top/bottom inner borders**, measure *width* of quilt top center (including added borders). Trim **top/bottom inner borders** to determined length. Matching centers and corners, sew **top/bottom inner borders** to quilt top.

Center and stitch **top pieced border** to top edge of quilt, beginning and ending seams exactly $1/4"$ from each corner of quilt top. Backstitch at beginning and ending of stitching to reinforce. In the same manner, sew **bottom** and **side pieced borders** to quilt top.

Fold one corner of quilt top diagonally with right sides together, matching outer edges of **pieced borders** as shown in **Fig. 2**. Beginning at point where previous seams end, sew **borders** together, backstitching at beginning and end of seam. Repeat to sew remaining **pieced border** corners together.

Repeat Steps 1 – 2 to sew **side**, **top**, and then **bottom outer borders** to quilt.

Border Unit
(make 114)

Corner Border Unit
(make 4)

Top/Bottom Pieced Border
(make 2)

Side Pieced Border
(make 2)

Fig. 2

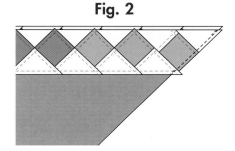

COMPLETING THE QUILT

1. Follow **Quilting**, page 53, to mark, layer, and quilt as desired. Our entire quilt is hand quilted "in the ditch."

2. Cut a 34" square of binding fabric. Follow **Binding**, page 60, to bind quilt using $2^1/_2$"w bias binding with mitered corners.

Quilt Assembly Diagram

"*My* mama always said you should learn how to do something just the way you were going to be doing it for life. Start on something you don't care a thing about, and you'll never finish and never learn what you need."

—Helen Henry, Endless Chain

Patriotic Sampler

$\mathscr{B}$y the time the ladies of the SCC Bee were quilting their third Patriotic Sampler quilt, they felt a spirit of unity as never before. Their friendships had deepened, and they had learned to share their burdens in order to make them lighter. And they even learned that compromise can be a thing of beauty.

Finished Quilt Size: 75" x 89" (191 cm x 226 cm)
Finished Block Size: 12" x 12" (30 cm x 30 cm)

·TTING AND ASSEMBLING THE BLOCKS

·low **Rotary Cutting**, page 48, to cut fabric. All measurements include a
·" seam allowance. Follow **Piecing and Pressing**, page 49, to assemble
·cks. There are two variations of each Block—a bright variation and a
·rk variation.

·OCK A

·e instructions for **Block A** are for **Variation 1**. For **Variation 2**, change
· to blue and blue to red.

·tting Block A
·m red print fabric:
- Cut 4 **large rectangles** $2^1/2$" x $8^1/2$".

·m cream print fabric:
- Cut 1 **large square** $4^1/2$" x $4^1/2$".
- Cut 8 **small squares** $2^1/2$" x $2^1/2$".

·m blue print fabric:
- Cut 8 **small squares** $2^1/2$" x $2^1/2$".
- Cut 4 **small rectangles** $2^1/2$" x $4^1/2$".

*⊘athy Adams reported that together we have pieced a total of sixty twelve-inch blocks
·ed, white, and blue prints, and from these we have assembled three sampler quilts —
·e more expertly than others. We hope to raise as much as two thousand dollars auctioning*

*the quilts at the annual Fourth
of July picnic. We set to work
quilting our third sampler. We
were grateful for the work and
the companionship."*

*—Minutes from the SCC Bee,
June 9, 2004,
Endless Chain*

YARDAGE REQUIREMENTS
*Yardage is based
on 43"/44"
(109 cm/112 cm)
wide fabric. Yardage
for blocks will vary,
since any number of
color combinations
may be used. For
our quilt, we used
a combination of
bright and dark fat
quarters. A fat
quarter measures
approximately
18" x 22"
(46 cm x 56).*

Approximately 60 red,
cream, and blue print
fat quarters

$5/8$ yd (57 cm) of red
stripe fabric

$1^3/8$ yds (1.3 m)
of cream print

$2^3/8$ yds (2.2 m) of
blue print fabric

7 yds (6.4 m) of
backing fabric

1 yd (91 cm) of
binding fabric

*You will also need:
83" x 97"
(211 cm x 246 cm)
rectangle of batting*

Fig. 1

Fig. 2

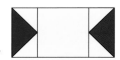

Flying Geese Unit (make 4)

Unit 1 (make 2)

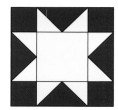

Unit 2

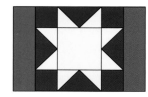

Unit 3

Unit 4 (make 2)

Unit 5

Block A, Variation 1

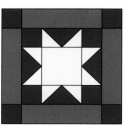

Block A, Variation 2

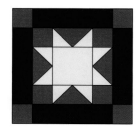

Strip Set (make 2)

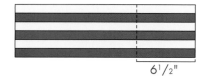

6^1/$_2$"

Unit 1 (make 4)

Block B

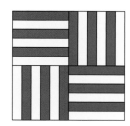

Making Block A

1. With right sides together, place 1 cream **small square** on 1 end of 1 **small rectangle** and stitch diagonally. Trim ^{1}/$_4$" from stitching line (**Fig. 1**). Open up and press, pressing seam allowance to darker fabric.

2. Place another cream **small square** on opposite end of **small rectangle**. Stitch and trim as shown in **Fig. 2**. Open up and press to complete **Flying Geese Unit**. Make 4 **Flying Geese Units**.

3. Sew 2 blue **small squares** and 1 **Flying Geese Unit** together to make **Unit 1**. Make 2 **Unit 1's**.

4. Sew 2 **Flying Geese Units** and **large square** together to make **Unit 2**.

5. Sew 2 **Unit 1's** and **Unit 2** together to make **Unit 3**.

6. Sew 1 **large rectangle** and 2 blue **small squares** together to make **Unit 4**. Make 2 **Unit 4's**.

7. Sew 2 **large rectangles** and **Unit 3** together to make **Unit 5**.

8. Sew 2 **Unit 4's** and **Unit 5** together to make **Block A, Variation 1**.

BLOCK B

Cutting Block B
From red print fabric:
- Cut 6 **strips** 1^1/$_2$" x 15".

From cream print fabric:
- Cut 6 **strips** 1^1/$_2$" x 15".

Making Block B

1. Alternating colors, sew 3 red **strips** and 3 cream **strips** together to make **Strip Set**. Make 2 **Strip Sets**. Cut **Strip Sets** at 6^1/$_2$" intervals to make 4 **Unit 1's**.

2. Rotating units as shown, sew **Unit 1's** together to make **Block B**.

LOCK C

*instructions for **Block C** are for **Variation 1**. For*
ariation 2, change red to blue and blue to red.

tting Block C
m red print fabric:
- Cut 4 **small squares** $3^1/_2$" x $3^1/_2$".

m cream print fabric:
- Cut 1 **large square** $6^1/_2$" x $6^1/_2$".
- Cut 8 **small squares** $3^1/_2$" x $3^1/_2$".

m blue print fabric:
- Cut 4 **small squares** $3^1/_2$" x $3^1/_2$".
- Cut 4 **rectangles** $3^1/_2$" x $6^1/_2$".

king Block C

With right sides together, place 1 red
small square on 1 corner of **large square** and
stitch diagonally. Trim $^1/_4$" from stitching line
(**Fig. 3**). Open up and press seam allowance
to darker fabric.

Continue adding red **small squares** to corners of
large square as shown in **Fig. 4**. Open up and
press to complete **Unit 1**.

With right sides together, place 1 cream **small
square** on 1 end of 1 **rectangle** and stitch
diagonally. Trim $^1/_4$" from stitching line (**Fig. 5**).
Open up and press, pressing seam allowance
to darker fabric.

Place another cream **small square** on opposite
end of **rectangle**. Stitch and trim as shown in
Fig. 6. Open up and press to complete **Flying
Geese Unit**. Make 4 **Flying Geese Units**.

Sew 2 blue **small squares** and 1 **Flying Geese
Unit** together to make **Unit 2**. Make 2 **Unit 2's**.

Sew 2 **Flying Geese Units** and **Unit 1** together to
make **Unit 3**.

Sew 2 **Unit 2's** and **Unit 3** together to make
Block C, Variation 1.

Fig. 3   Fig. 4

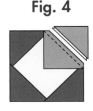

Unit 1

Fig. 5   Fig. 6

Flying Geese Unit
(make 4)

Unit 2
(make 2)

Unit 3

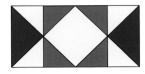

Block C, Variation 1   **Block C, Variation 2**

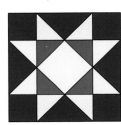
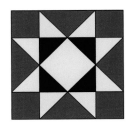

BLOCK D

Cutting Block D
From red print fabrics:
- Cut **strip #3** $1^1/2"$ x $3^1/2"$ and **strip #4** $1^1/2"$ x $4^1/2"$ from one print.
- Cut **strip #11** $1^1/2"$ x $7^1/2"$ and **strip #12** $1^1/2"$ x $8^1/2"$ from one print.
- Cut **strip #19** $1^1/2"$ x $11^1/2"$ and **strip #20** $1^1/2"$ x $12^1/2"$ from one print.

From cream print fabrics:
- Cut 1 **square** $2^1/2"$ x $2^1/2"$.
- Cut **strip #7** $1^1/2"$ x $5^1/2"$ and **strip #8** $1^1/2"$ x $6^1/2"$ from one print.
- Cut **strip #15** $1^1/2"$ x $9^1/2"$ and **strip #16** $1^1/2"$ x $10^1/2"$ from one print.

From blue print fabrics:
- Cut **strip #1** $1^1/2"$ x $2^1/2"$ and **strip #2** $1^1/2"$ x $3^1/2"$ from one print.
- Cut **strip #5** $1^1/2"$ x $4^1/2"$ and **strip #6** $1^1/2"$ x $5^1/2"$ from one print.
- Cut **strip #9** $1^1/2"$ x $6^1/2"$ and **strip #10** $1^1/2"$ x $7^1/2"$ from one print.
- Cut **strip #13** $1^1/2"$ x $8^1/2"$ and **strip #14** $1^1/2"$ x $9^1/2"$ from one print.
- Cut **strip #17** $1^1/2"$ x $10^1/2"$ and **strip #18** $1^1/2"$ x $11^1/2"$ from one print.

Making Block D
1. Sew **square** and **strip #1** together to make **Unit 1**.

2. Sew **strip #2** to right edge of **Unit 1** to make **Unit 2**.

3. Sew **strip #3** to bottom edge of **Unit 2** to make **Unit 3**.

4. Sew **strip #4** to left edge of **Unit 3** to make **Unit 4**.

5. Continuing sewing **strips** to **Unit 4** working clockwise and in numerical order as shown in **Block Assembly** to make **Block D**.

Unit 1   **Unit 2**

Unit 3   **Unit 4**

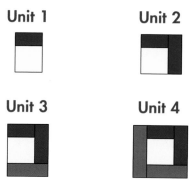

Block Assembly

Block D

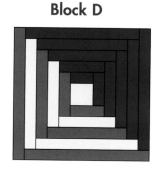

BLOCK E

Cutting Block E
From red print fabric:
- Cut 2 **strips** 2" x 21".

From cream print fabrics:
- Cut 2 **strips** 2" x 21".
- Cut 1 **large square** $3^1/2$" x $3^1/2$".
- Cut 8 **small squares** 2" x 2".

From blue print fabrics:
- Cut 4 **small squares** 2" x 2".
- Cut 4 **rectangles** 2" x $3^1/2$".

Making Block E

1. Alternating colors, sew **strips** together to make **Strip Set**. Cut **Strip Set** into **Unit 1**, $12^1/2$"l, and **Unit 2**, $6^1/2$"l.

2. With right sides together, place 1 cream **small square** on 1 end of 1 **rectangle** and stitch diagonally. Trim $1/4$" from stitching line (**Fig. 7**). Open up and press, pressing seam allowance to darker fabric.

3. Place another cream **small square** on opposite end of **rectangle**. Stitch and trim as shown in **Fig. 8**. Open up and press to complete **Flying Geese Unit**. Make 4 **Flying Geese Units**.

4. Sew 2 blue **small squares** and 1 **Flying Geese Unit** together to make **Unit 3**. Make 2 **Unit 3's**.

5. Sew 2 **Flying Geese Units** and **large square** together to make **Unit 4**.

6. Sew 2 **Unit 3's** and **Unit 4** together to make **Unit 5**.

7. Sew **Unit 5** and **Unit 2** together to make **Unit 6**.

8. Sew **Unit 6** and **Unit 1** together to make **Block E**.

Strip Set

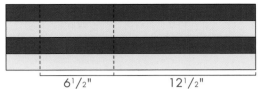

$6^1/2$" $12^1/2$"

Unit 1   **Unit 2**

Fig. 7   **Fig. 8**

Flying Geese Unit (make 4)   **Unit 3** (make 2)

Unit 4   **Unit 5**

Unit 6

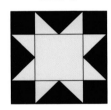
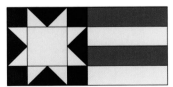

Block E

Fig. 9

Triangle-Squares
(make 4)

Unit 1

Fig. 10

Fig. 11

Flying Geese Unit
(make 4)

Unit 2
(make 2)

Unit 3

Block F, Variation 1

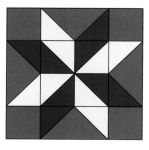

Block F, Variation 2

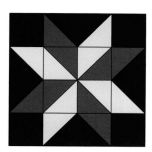

BLOCK F

*The instructions for **Block F** are for **Variation 1**. For Variation 2, change red to blue, cream to red, and blue to cream.*

Cutting Block F
From red print fabric:
- Cut 4 **small squares** $3^1/_2$" x $3^1/_2$".
- Cut 4 **rectangles** $3^1/_2$" x $6^1/_2$".

From cream print fabric:
- Cut 4 **small squares** $3^1/_2$" x $3^1/_2$".
- Cut 2 **large squares** $3^7/_8$" x $3^7/_8$".

From blue print fabric:
- Cut 4 **small squares** $3^1/_2$" x $3^1/_2$".
- Cut 2 **large squares** $3^7/_8$" x $3^7/_8$".

Making Block F
1. Draw diagonal line (corner to corner) on wrong side of each cream **large square**. With right sides together, place 1 cream **large square** on top of 1 blue **large square**. Stitch seam $1/_4$" from each side of drawn line (**Fig. 9**)

2. Cut along drawn line and press seam allowance to darker fabric to make 2 **Triangle-Squares**. Make 4 **Triangle-Squares**.

3. Sew 4 **Triangle-Squares** together to make **Unit 1**.

4. With right sides together, place 1 blue **small square** on left end of 1 **rectangle** and stitch diagonally. Trim $1/_4$" from stitching line (**Fig. 10**). Open up and press, pressing seam allowance to darker fabric.

5. Place 1 cream **small square** on right end of **rectangle**. Stitch and trim as shown in **Fig. 11**. Open up and press to complete **Flying Geese Unit**. Make 4 **Flying Geese Units**.

6. Sew 2 red **small squares** and 1 **Flying Geese Unit** together to make **Unit 2**. Make 2 **Unit 2's**.

7. Sew 2 **Flying Geese Units** and **Unit 1** together to make **Unit 3**.

8. Sew 2 **Unit 2's** and **Unit 3** together to make **Block F, Variation 1**.

40

BLOCK G

The instructions for **Block G** are for **Variation 1**. For **Variation 2**, change the center cream large square to blue and the blue large squares to cream.

Cutting Block G

From red print fabric:
- Cut 8 **strips** $1\frac{1}{2}$" x $6\frac{1}{2}$".

From cream print fabric:
- Cut 4 **strips** $1\frac{1}{2}$" x $6\frac{1}{2}$".
- Cut 1 **large square** $3\frac{1}{2}$" x $3\frac{1}{2}$".
- Cut 8 **small squares** 2" x 2".

From blue print fabric:
- Cut 4 **large squares** $3\frac{1}{2}$" x $3\frac{1}{2}$".
- Cut 4 **small squares** 2" x 2".
- Cut 4 **rectangles** 2" x $3\frac{1}{2}$".

Making Block G

With right sides together, place 1 cream **small square** on 1 end of 1 **rectangle** and stitch diagonally. Trim $\frac{1}{4}$" from stitching line (**Fig. 12**). Open up and press, pressing seam allowance to darker fabric.

Place a cream **small square** on opposite end of **rectangle**. Stitch and trim as shown in **Fig. 13**. Open up and press to complete **Flying Geese Unit**. Make 4 **Flying Geese Units**.

Sew 2 blue **small squares** and 1 **Flying Geese Unit** together to make **Unit 1**. Make 2 **Unit 1's**.

Sew 2 **Flying Geese Units** and 1 cream **large square** together to make **Unit 2**.

Sew 2 **Unit 1's** and **Unit 2** together to make **Unit 3**.

Sew 2 red **strips** and 1 cream **strip** together to make **Unit 4**. Make 4 **Unit 4's**.

Sew 2 blue **large squares** and 1 **Unit 4** together to make **Unit 5**. Make 2 **Unit 5's**.

Sew 2 **Unit 4's** and **Unit 3** together to make **Unit 6**.

Sew 2 **Unit 5's** and **Unit 6** together to make **Block G, Variation 1**.

Fig. 12 **Fig. 13**

Flying Geese Unit
(make 4)

Unit 1
(make 2)

Unit 2 **Unit 3**

Unit 4
(make 4)

Unit 5
(make 2)

Unit 6

Block G, Variation 1

Block G, Variation 2

Fig. 14

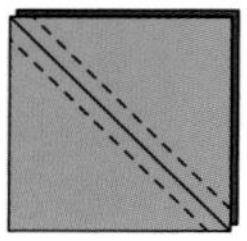

Triangle-Squares
(make 4)

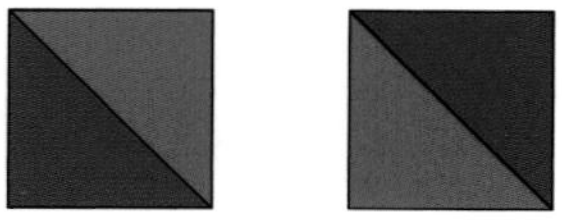

Fig. 15

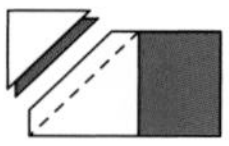

Fig. 16

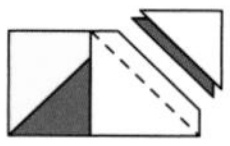

**Flying Geese
Unit A**
(make 4)

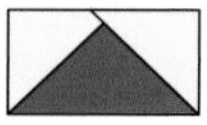

**Flying Geese
Unit B**
(make 4)

Unit 1
(make 4)

Unit 2
(make 2)

Unit 3

Block H, Variation 1

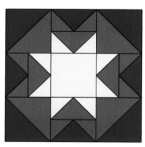

Block H, Variation 2

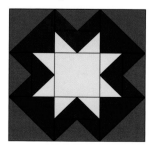

BLOCK H

*The instructions for **Block H** are for **Variation 1**. For **Variation 2**, change red to blue and blue to red.*

Cutting Block H
From red print fabric:
- Cut 2 **large squares** $4^7/8$" x $4^7/8$".
- Cut 8 **small squares** $2^1/2$" x $2^1/2$".
- Cut 4 **rectangles** $2^1/2$" x $4^1/2$".

From cream print fabric:
- Cut 1 **medium square** $4^1/2$" x $4^1/2$".
- Cut 8 **small squares** $2^1/2$" x $2^1/2$".

From blue print fabric:
- Cut 2 **large squares** $4^7/8$" x $4^7/8$".
- Cut 4 **rectangles** $2^1/2$" x $4^1/2$".

Making Block H

1. Draw diagonal line (corner to corner) on wrong sid[e] each red **large square**. With right sides together, p[l] 1 red **large square** on top of 1 blue **large square**. Stitch seam $1/4$" from each side of drawn line (**Fig.**

2. Cut along drawn line and press seam allowance[s] darker fabric to make 2 **Triangle-Squares**. Make 4 **Triangle-Squares**.

3. With right sides together, place 1 cream **small squ[are]** on 1 end of 1 red **rectangle** and stitch diagonally. Trim $1/4$" from stitching line (**Fig. 15**). Open up and press, pressing seam allowance to darker fabric.

4. Place another cream **small square** on opposite e[nd] of **rectangle**. Stitch and trim as shown in **Fig. 16**. Open up and press to complete **Flying Geese Unit A**. Make 4 **Flying Geese Unit A's**.

5. Repeat Steps 3 – 4 using red **small squares** and blue **rectangles** to make 4 **Flying Geese Unit B's**.

6. Sew 1 **Flying Geese Unit A** and 1 **Flying Geese Unit B** together to make **Unit 1**. Make 4 **Unit 1's**.

7. Sew 2 **Triangle-Squares** and 1 **Unit 1** together to make **Unit 2**. Make 2 **Unit 2's**.

8. Sew 2 **Unit 1's** and **medium square** together to make **Unit 3**.

9. Sew 2 **Unit 2's** and **Unit 3** together to make **Bloc[k H]** **Variation 1**.

BLOCK I

The instructions for **Block I** are for **Variation 1**. For **Variation 2**, change cream small and medium squares to blue, red small and medium squares to cream, and blue small squares and rectangles to red.

Cutting Block I

From red print fabric:
- Cut 3 **narrow strips** $1^1/2$" x 21".
- Cut 1 **wide strip** $2^1/2$" x 21".
- Cut 4 **large squares** $2^3/8$" x $2^3/8$".
- Cut 8 **small squares** 2" x 2".

From cream print fabric:
- Cut 3 **narrow strips** $1^1/2$" x 21".
- Cut 1 **wide strip** $2^1/2$" x 21".
- Cut 4 **large squares** $2^3/8$" x $2^3/8$".
- Cut 8 **small squares** 2" x 2".

From blue print fabric:
- Cut 8 **small squares** 2" x 2".
- Cut 8 **rectangles** 2" x $3^1/2$".

Making Block I

Alternating colors, sew **wide** and **narrow strips** together (**wide strips** should be on outer edges) to make **Strip Set**. Cut 2 squares $6^1/2$" x $6^1/2$" (turned on point) as shown to make 2 **Unit 1's**.

Draw diagonal line (corner to corner) on wrong side of each cream **large square**. With right sides together, place 1 cream **large square** on top of 1 red **large square**. Stitch seam $1/4$" from each side of drawn line (**Fig. 17**)

Cut along drawn line and press seam allowance to darker fabric to make 2 **Triangle-Squares**. Make 8 **Triangle-Squares**.

Sew 4 **Triangle-Squares** together to make **Unit 2**. Make 2 **Unit 2's**.

With right sides together, place 1 cream **small square** on left end of 1 **rectangle** and stitch diagonally. Trim $1/4$" from stitching line (**Fig. 18**). Open up and press, pressing seam allowance to darker fabric.

Place 1 red **small square** on right end of **rectangle**. Stitch and trim as shown in **Fig. 19**. Open up and press to complete **Flying Geese Unit**. Make 8 **Flying Geese Units**.

Strip Set

Unit 1
(make 2)

Fig. 17

Triangle-Squares
(make 8)

Unit 2
(make 2)

Fig. 18   **Fig. 19**

Flying Geese Unit
(make 8)

Unit 3
(make 4)

Unit 4
(make 2)

Unit 5
(make 2)

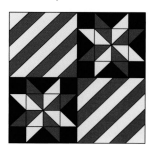

Block I, Variation 1

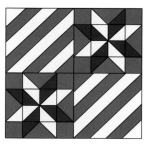

Block I, Variation 2

Fig. 20

Triangle-Squares
(make 4)

Unit 1

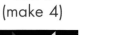

7. Sew 2 blue **small squares** and 1 **Flying Geese Unit** together to make **Unit 3**. Make 4 **Unit 3's**.

8. Sew 2 **Flying Geese Units** and 1 **Unit 2** together to make **Unit 4**. Make 2 **Unit 4's**.

9. Sew 2 **Unit 3's** and 1 **Unit 4** together to make **Unit 5**. Make 2 **Unit 5's**.

10. Sew 2 **Unit 1's** and 2 **Unit 5's** together to make **Block I, Variation 1.**

BLOCK J

*The instructions for **Block J** are for **Variation 1**. For **Variation 2**, change red to blue and blue to red.*

Cutting Block J
From red print fabric:
- Cut 4 **small squares** $3^1/_2$" x $3^1/_2$".
- Cut 4 **rectangles** $3^1/_2$" x $6^1/_2$".

From cream print fabric:
- Cut 2 **large squares** $3^7/_8$" x $3^7/_8$".
- Cut 8 **small squares** $3^1/_2$" x $3^1/_2$".

From blue print fabric:
- Cut 2 **large squares** $3^7/_8$" x $3^7/_8$".

Making Block J
1. Draw diagonal line (corner to corner) on wrong side of each cream **large square**. With right sides together, place 1 cream **large square** on top of 1 blue **large square**. Stitch seam $1/_4$" from each side of drawn line (**Fig. 20**)

2. Cut along drawn line and press seam allowance to darker fabric to make 2 **Triangle-Squares**. Make 4 **Triangle-Squares**.

3. Sew 4 **Triangle-Squares** together to make **Unit 1**.

44

4. With right sides together, place 1 cream **small square** on 1 end of 1 **rectangle** and stitch diagonally. Trim ¹/₄" from stitching line (**Fig. 21**). Open up and press, pressing seam allowance to darker fabric.

5. Place another cream **small square** on opposite end of **rectangle**. Stitch and trim as shown in **Fig. 22**. Open up and press to complete **Flying Geese Unit**. Make 4 **Flying Geese Units**.

6. Sew 2 red **small squares** and 1 **Flying Geese Unit** together to make **Unit 2**. Make 2 **Unit 2's**.

7. Sew 2 **Flying Geese Units** and 1 **Unit 1** together to make **Unit 3**.

8. Sew 2 **Unit 2's** and **Unit 3** together to make **Block J, Variation 1**.

CUTTING OUT THE SASHINGS AND BORDERS

All strips are cut across the width of the fabric unless otherwise noted. Borders include an extra 4" of length for "insurance" and will be trimmed after assembling quilt top center. All other measurements include a ¹/₄" seam allowance.

From red stripe fabric for inner borders:
- Cut 8 **inner border strips** 2¹/₂"w.

From cream print fabric:
- Cut 17 strips 2¹/₂"w. From these strips, cut 49 **sashing strips** 2¹/₂" x 12¹/₂".

From blue print fabric:
- Cut 2 *lengthwise* **side outer borders** 6¹/₂" x 80¹/₂".
- Cut 2 *lengthwise* **top/bottom outer borders** 6¹/₂" x 78¹/₂".

From remaining width:
- Cut 6 strips 2¹/₂"w. From these strips, cut 30 **sashing squares** 2¹/₂" x 2¹/₂".

Fig. 21

Fig. 22

Flying Geese Unit (make 4)

Unit 2 (make 2)

Unit 3

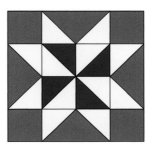

Block J, Variation 1

Block J, Variation 2

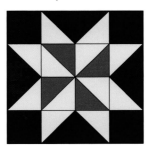

45

Row
(make 5)

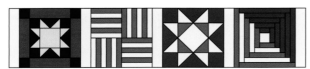

Sashing Row
(make 6)

Quilt Top Diagram

ASSEMBLING THE QUILT TOP CEN

*Once blocks are completed, arrange
blocks on floor, balancing colors and
designs to achieve desired look.*

1.   Sew 4 **Blocks** and 5 **sashing strips**
     together to make **Row**. Make 5 **Ro**

2.   Sew 4 **sashing strips** and 5 **sash
     squares** together to make **Sashin
     Row**. Make 6 **Sashing Rows**.

3.   Alternating **Sashing Rows** and **R**
     sew **Sashing Rows** and **Rows**
     together to complete quilt top ce

ADDING THE BORDERS

*Refer to **Quilt Top Diagram** for placer*

1.   Sew 2 **inner border strips** togeth
     end to end to make **inner border**
     Make 4 **inner borders**.

2.   To determine length of **side inner
     borders**, measure *length* of quilt
     center. Trim 2 **inner borders** to
     determined length. Matching ce
     and corners, sew **side inner bord**
     to quilt top.

3.   To determine length of **top/botto**
     inner borders, measure *width* of
     top center (including added bord
     Trim remaining **inner borders** to
     determined length. Matching cen
     and corners, sew **top/bottom inn**
     borders to quilt top.

4.   Repeat Steps 2 – 3 to sew **outer**
     borders to quilt top.

COMPLETING THE QUILT

1. Follow **Quilting**, page 53, to mark, layer, and quilt as desired.

2. Cut a 31" square from fabric for binding. Follow **Binding**, page 60, to bind quilt using $2^1/2$"w bias binding with mitered corners.

General Instructions

Complete instructions are given for making each of the projects shown in this book. To make your project easier and more enjoyable, we encourage you to carefully read all the general instructions, study the color photographs, and familiarize yourself with the individual project instructions before beginning a project.

Fig. 1

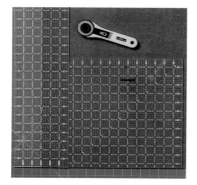

Fig. 2

Fig. 3

ROTARY CUTTING

Rotary cutting has brought speed and accuracy to quiltmaking by allowing quilters to easily cut strips of fabric and then cut those strips into smaller pieces.

- Place fabric on work surface with fold closest to you.

- Cut all strips from the selvage-to-selvage width of the fabric unless otherwise indicated in project instructions.

- Square left edge of fabric using rotary cutter and rulers (**Figs. 1 – 2**).

- To cut each strip required for a project, place the ruler over the cut edge of the fabric, aligning desired marking on the ruler with the cut edge (**Fig. 3**); make the cut.

- When cutting several strips from a single piece of fabric, it is important to make sure that cuts remain at a perfect right angle to the fold; square fabric as needed.

TEMPLATE CUTTING

Our piecing template patterns include a $^1/_4$" seam allowance. Patterns for appliqué templates do not include seam allowances. When cutting instructions say to cut in reverse, place the template upside down on the fabric to cut piece in reverse.

1. To make a template from a pattern, use a permanent fine-point pen to carefully trace the pattern onto template plastic, making sure to transfer all markings. Cut out template along outer drawn line. Check template against original pattern for accuracy.
2. To use a piecing template, place template on wrong side of fabric (unless otherwise indicated), aligning grain line on template with straight grain of fabric. Use a sharp fabric marking pencil to draw around template. Cut out fabric piece using scissors or rotary cutting equipment.
3. To use appliqué templates, place template on right side of fabric. Use a mechanical pencil with a very fine lead to draw around template on fabric. Use scissors to cut out appliqué a scant $^1/_4$" outside drawn line.

PIECING AND PRESSING

Precise cutting, followed by accurate piecing and careful pressing, will ensure that all the pieces of your quilt top fit together well.

PIECING

- Set sewing machine stitch length for approximately 11 stitches per inch.

- Use a neutral-colored general-purpose sewing thread (not quilting thread) in the needle and in the bobbin.

- An accurate $^1/_4$" seam allowance is **essential**. Presser feet that are $^1/_4$" wide are available for most sewing machines.

- When piecing, always place pieces **right sides** together and match raw edges; pin if necessary.

- Chain piecing saves time and will usually result in more accurate piecing.

- Trim away points of seam allowances that extend beyond edges of sewn seams.

Fig. 4

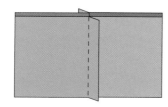

Fig. 5

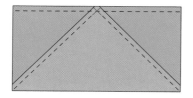

Fig. 6

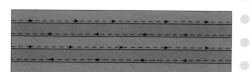

Sewing Across Seam Intersections

When sewing across the intersection of two seams, place pieces right sides together and match seams exactly, making sure seam allowances are pressed in opposite directions (**Fig. 4**).

Sewing Sharp Points

To ensure sharp points when joining triangular or diagonal pieces, stitch across the center of the "X" (shown in pink) formed on the wrong side by previous seams (**Fig. 5**).

Sewing Strip Sets

When there are several strips to assemble into a strip set, first sew the strips together into pairs, then sew the pairs together to form the strip set. To help avoid distortion, sew 1 seam in 1 direction and then sew the next seam in the opposite direction (**Fig. 6**). Take special care not to stretch strips.

PRESSING

- Use a steam iron set on "Cotton" for all pressing.

- Press after sewing each seam.

- Seam allowances are almost always pressed to one side, usually toward the darker fabric. However, to reduce bulk it may occasionally be necessary to press seam allowances toward the lighter fabric or even to press them open.

- To prevent a dark fabric seam allowance from showing through a light fabric, trim the darker seam allowance slightly narrower than the lighter seam allowance.

- To press long seams, such as those in long strip sets, without curving or other distortion, lay strips across the width of the ironing board.

PLIQUÉ

dle-Turn Appliqué

is traditional hand appliqué method, the needle is used to turn eam allowance under as you sew the appliqué to the ground fabric using a Blind Stitch, page 63 (**Fig. 31**). When ing, match the color of thread to the color of appliqué to uise your stitches. Appliqué each piece starting with the ones tly on the background fabric. It is not necessary to appliqué s that will be covered by another appliqué. Stitches on the right of fabric should not show. Clipped areas should be secured with w extra stitches to prevent fraying.

Place template on right side of appliqué fabric. Use a mechanical pencil with a very fine lead to lightly draw around template, leaving at least $1/2$" between shapes; repeat for number of appliqués specified in project instructions.
Cut out shapes a scant $1/4$" outside drawn line. Arrange shapes on background fabric and pin or baste in place.
Thread a sharps needle with a single strand of general-purpose sewing thread the color of the appliqué; knot one end.
Pin center of appliqué to right side of background fabric. Begin on as straight an edge as possible and use point of needle to turn under a small amount of seam allowance, concealing drawn line on appliqué. Blindstitch appliqué to the background, turning under the seam allowance. Clip inside curves and points up to, but not through, drawn line as you stitch.

paring Fusible Appliqués

erns for fused appliqués are printed in reverse to enable you se our speedy method of preparing appliqués by following s 1 – 3 (below). White or light-colored fabrics may need e lined with fusible interfacing before applying fusible web revent darker fabrics from showing through.

Place paper-backed fusible web, web side down, over appliqué pattern. Use a pencil to trace pattern onto paper side of web as many times as indicated in project instructions for a single fabric.
Follow manufacturer's instructions to fuse traced patterns to wrong side of fabrics. Do not remove paper backing.
Use scissors to cut out appliqué pieces along traced lines.
Remove paper backing from all pieces.

"*That's my mama's machine, made back in the early 1900's. Every quilt she made, she made on that machine. Never wanted anything different. Never needed anything better. She used that and kept her family warm.*"

— Helen Henry, Endless Chain

"Elisa touched the last quilt Nancy took out and felt as if she had come home. Tiny vertical strips in bright colors met horizontal strips in a variety of lengths and widths. 'You did this by hand? All by hand? And the colors? This is a rainbow. This would keep anybody warm, wouldn't it? Like sunbeams.'"

—from Endless Chain

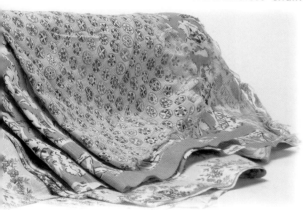

Machine Decorative Stitch Appliqué

Some sewing machines feature a Blanket Stitch simila the one used in this book. Refer to your Owner's Man for machine set-up. If your machine does not have this stitch, try any of the decorative stitches your machine until you are satisfied with the look.

1. Thread sewing machine and bobbin with general-purpose thread.
2. Arrange appliqué pieces on background fabric a described in project instructions. Fuse appliqués i place.
3. Pin a stabilizer, such as paper or any of the commercially available products, on wrong side background fabric before stitching appliqués in place.
4. Begin by stitching two or three stitches in place (d feed dogs or set stitch length at 0) to anchor three Most of the decorative stitch should be done on t appliqué with the right edges of the stitch falling the very outside edge of the appliqué. Stitch over exposed raw edges of appliqué pieces.
5. For outside corners, stitch just past the corner, stopping with the needle in background fabric. Ra presser foot. Pivot project, lower presser foot, and stitch adjacent side.
6. For inside corners, stitch just past the corner, stopping with the needle in background fabric. Ra presser foot. Pivot project, lower presser foot, and stitch adjacent side.
7. When stitching outside curves, stop with needle in background fabric. Raise presser foot and pivot project as needed. Lower presser foot and continu stitching, pivoting as often as necessary to follow curve.
8. When stitching inside curves, stop with needle in background fabric. Raise presser foot and pivot project as needed. Lower presser foot and continu stitching, pivoting as often as necessary to follow curve.
9. Do not backstitch at end of stitching. Pull threads t wrong side of background fabric; knot thread and trim ends.
10. Carefully tear away stabilizer.

QUILTING

*Quilting holds the three layers (top, batting, and backing) of the quilt together and can be done by hand or machine. Because marking, layering, and quilting are interrelated and may be done in different orders depending on circumstances, please read the entire **Quilting** section, pages 53 — 59, before beginning project.*

TYPES OF QUILTING
In the Ditch Quilting
Quilting along seamlines or along edges of appliquéd pieces is called "in the ditch" quilting. This type of quilting should be done on the side **opposite** the seam allowance and does not need to be marked.

Outline Quilting
Quilting a consistent distance, usually $^1/_4$", from a seam or appliqué is called "outline" quilting. Outline quilting may be marked, or $^1/_4$"w masking tape may be placed along seamlines for a quilting guide. (Do not leave tape on quilt longer than necessary, since it may leave an adhesive residue.)

Motif Quilting
Quilting a design, such as a feathered wreath is called "motif" quilting. This type of quilting should be marked before basting quilt layers together.

Echo Quilting
Quilting that follows the outline of an appliquéd or pieced design with two or more parallel lines is called "echo" quilting. This type of quilting does not need to be marked.

Channel Quilting
Quilting with straight, parallel lines is called "channel" quilting. This type of quilting may be marked or stitched using a guide.

Crosshatch Quilting
Quilting straight lines in a grid pattern is called "crosshatch" quilting. Lines may be stitched parallel to edges of quilt or stitched diagonally. This type of quilting may be marked or stitched using a guide.

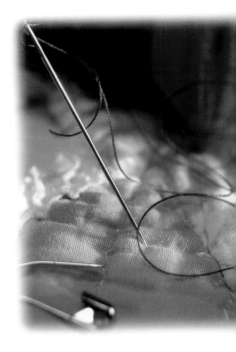

"Nancy pulled out a quilt and held it in front of her. 'This is a new one. Mama calls it Oklahoma Made a Monkey Out of Me. This is a Monkey Wrench pattern,' Nancy explained. 'And this is the Road to Oklahoma block. See the unique way she combined them? And if you look carefully, you'll see monkeys in lots of the prints.'"

—from Endless Chain

Meandering Quilting

Quilting in random curved lines and swirls is called "meandering" quilting. Quilting lines should not cross touch each other. This type of quilting does not need to marked.

Stipple Quilting

Meandering quilting that is very closely spaced is calle "stipple" quilting. Stippling will flatten the area quilted is often stitched in background areas to raise appliqué pieced designs. This type of quilting does not need to marked.

MARKING QUILTING LINES

Quilting lines may be marked using fabric marking pencils, chalk markers, water- or air-soluble pens, or le pencils.

Simple quilting designs may be marked with chalk or chalk pencil after basting. A small area may be marked then quilted, before moving to next area to be marked. Intricate designs should be marked before basting using a more durable marker.

Caution: Pressing may permanently set some marks. Tes different markers **on scrap fabric** to find one that marks clearly and can be thoroughly removed.

A wide variety of precut quilting stencils, as well as enti books of quilting patterns, are available. Using a stenci makes it easier to mark intricate or repetitive designs or your quilt top.

To make a stencil from a pattern, center template plastic over pattern and use a permanent marker to trace patte onto plastic. Use a craft knife with a single or double blade to cut narrow slits along traced lines (**Fig. 7**). Use desired marking tool and stencil to mark quilting lines.

Fig. 7

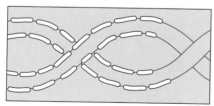

CHOOSING AND PREPARING THE BACKING

To allow for slight shifting of the quilt top during quilting, the backing should be approximately 4" larger on all sides than the quilt top for bed-sized quilts and large wall hangings and 2" larger for small wall hangings. Yardage requirements listed for quilt backings are calculated for 43"/44"w fabric. If you are making a bed-size quilt, using 90"w or 108"w fabric for the backing may eliminate piecing. To piece a backing using 43"/44"w fabric, use the following instructions.

Measure length and width of quilt top; add 8" (4") to each measurement.

If determined width is less than 80", cut the backing fabric into two lengths slightly longer than the determined *length* measurement. Trim selvages. Place lengths with right sides facing and sew long edges together, forming a tube (**Fig. 8**). Match seams and press along 1 fold (**Fig. 9**). Cut along pressed fold to form a single piece (**Fig. 10**).

If determined width is 80" or more, cut backing fabric into three lengths slightly longer than determined *width* measurement. Trim selvages. Sew long edges together to form single piece.

Trim backing to correct size, if necessary, and press seam allowances open.

Fig. 8

Fig. 9

Fig. 10

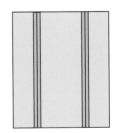

CHOOSING AND PREPARING THE BATTING

Choosing the right batting will make your quilting job easier. The projects in this book are made using cotton batting which does not require tight quilting. If machine quilting, choose a low-loft all cotton or cotton/polyester blend batting because the cotton helps "grip" the layers of the quilt. For hand quilting, choose a low-loft batting in any of the fiber types described here.

Batting options include cotton/polyester batting, which combines the best of both polyester and cotton battings; fusible battings which do not need to be basted before quilting; bonded polyester which is treated with a protective coating to stabilize the fibers and to reduce "bearding," a process in which batting fibers work their way out through the quilt fabrics; and wool and silk battings, which are generally more expensive and usually only dry-cleanable.

Whichever batting you choose, read the manufacturer's instructions closely for any special notes on care or preparation. When you're ready to use your chosen batting in a project, cut batting the same size as the prepared backing.

Fig. 11

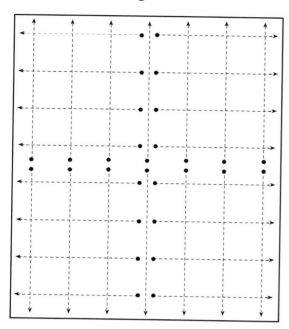

ASSEMBLING THE QUILT

1. Examine wrong side of quilt top closely; trim any seam allowances and clip any threads that may show through the front of the quilt. Press quilt top.

2. If quilt top is to be marked before layering, mark quilting lines (see **Marking Quilting Lines**, page 54).

3. Place backing wrong side up on a flat surface. Use masking tape to tape edges of backing to surface. Place batting on top of backing fabric. Smooth batting gently, being careful not to stretch or tear. Center quilt top right side up on batting.

4. If hand quilting, begin in the center and work toward the outer edges to hand baste all layers together. Use long stitches and place basting lines approximately 4" apart (**Fig. 11**). Smooth fullness or wrinkles toward outer edges.

5. If machine quilting, use 1" rustproof safety pins to "pin-baste" all layers together, spacing pins approximately 4" apart. Begin at the center and work toward the outer edges to secure all layers. If possible, place pins away from areas that will be quilted, although pins may be removed as needed when quilting.

HAND QUILTING

The quilting stitch is a basic running stitch that forms a broken line on the quilt top and backing. Stitches on the quilt top and backing should be straight and equal in length.

Fig. 12

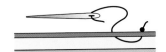

Fig. 13

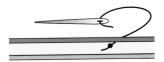

Fig. 14

1. Secure center of quilt in hoop or frame. Check quilt top and backing to make sure they are smooth. To help prevent puckers, always begin quilting in the center of the quilt and work toward the outside edges.
2. Thread needle with an 18" — 20" length of quilting thread; knot one end. Using a thimble, insert needle into quilt top and batting approximately $1/2$" from where you wish to begin quilting. Bring needle up at the point where you wish to begin (**Fig. 12**); when knot catches on quilt top, give thread a quick, short pull to "pop" knot through fabric into batting (**Fig. 13**).
3. Holding the needle with your sewing hand and placing your other hand underneath the quilt, use thimble to push the tip of the needle down through all layers. As soon as needle touches your finger underneath, use that finger to push the tip of the needle only back up through the layers to top of quilt. (The amount of the needle showing above the fabric determines the length of the quilting stitch.) Referring to **Fig. 14**, rock the needle up and down, taking three to six stitches before bringing the needle and thread completely through the layers. Check the back of the quilt to make sure stitches are going through all layers. When quilting through a seam allowance or quilting a curve or corner, you may need to make one stitch at a time.
4. When you reach the end of your thread, knot thread close to the fabric and "pop" knot into batting; clip thread close to fabric.
5. Stop and move your hoop as often as necessary. You do not have to tie a knot every time you move your hoop; you may leave the thread dangling and pick it up again when you return to that part of the quilt.

STRAIGHT-LINE MACHINE QUILTING

The following instructions are for straight-line quilting, which requires a walking foot or even-feed foot. The term "straight-line" is somewhat deceptive, since curves (especially gentle ones) as well as straight lines can be stitched with this technique.

1. Using the same color general-purpose thread in the needle and bobbin avoids "dots" of bobbin thread being pulled to the surface.

2. Using general-purpose thread which matches the backing in the bobbin will add pattern and dimension to the quilt back without adding contrasting color. Refer to your owner's manual for recommended tension settings.

3. Set the stitch length for 6 – 10 stitches per inch and attach the walking foot to sewing machine.

4. After pin-basting, decide which section of the quilt will have the longest continuous quilting line, oftentimes the area from center top to center bottom. Leaving the area exposed where you will place your first line of quilting, roll up each edge of the quilt to help reduce the bulk, keeping fabrics smooth. Smaller projects may not need to be rolled.

5. Start stitching at beginning of longest quilting line, using very short stitches for the first $1/4$" to "lock" beginning of quilting line. Stitch across project, using one hand on each side of the walking foot to slightly spread the fabric and to guide the fabric through the machine. Lock stitches at end of quilting line.

6. Continue machine quilting, stitching longer quilting lines first to stabilize the quilt before moving on to other areas.

E-MOTION MACHINE QUILTING

motion quilting may be free form or may follow
rked quilting pattern.

Using the same color general-purpose thread in the needle
and bobbin avoids "dots" of bobbin thread being pulled to
the surface. Use general-purpose thread in the bobbin and
decorative thread for stitching, such as metallic, variegated
or contrasting-colored general-purpose thread, when you
desire the quilting to be more pronounced.

Use a darning foot and drop or cover feed dogs. Pull up
bobbin thread and hold both thread ends while you stitch
two or three stitches in place to lock thread. Cut threads
near quilt surface.

Place hands lightly on quilt on either side of darning foot to
slightly spread fabric and to move fabric through the
machine. Even stitch length is achieved by using smooth,
flowing hand motion and steady machine speed. Slow
machine speed and fast hand movement will create long
stitches. Fast machine speed and slow hand movement will
create short stitches. Move quilt sideways, back and forth,
in a circular motion, or in a random motion to create the
desired designs; do not rotate quilt. Lock stitches at the end
of each quilting line.

KING A HANGING SLEEVE

ching a hanging sleeve to the back of your wall hanging or
before the binding is added allows you to display your
pleted project on a wall.

Measure width of quilt top edge and subtract 1". Cut piece
of fabric 7" wide by the determined measurement.

Press short edges of fabric piece 1/4" to wrong side; press
edges 1/4" to wrong side again and machine stitch in
place.

Matching wrong sides, fold piece in half lengthwise to form
a tube.

Match raw edges and stitch hanging sleeve to center top
edge on back of wall hanging.

Bind wall hanging, treating the hanging sleeve as part of
the backing.

Blindstitch bottom of hanging sleeve to backing, taking care
not to stitch through to front of quilt.

Fig. 15

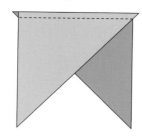

Fig. 16

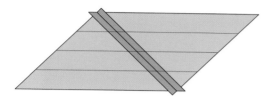

Fig. 17

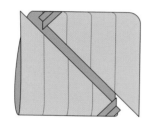

Fig. 18

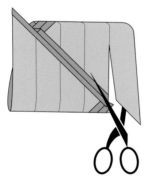

BINDING

Binding encloses the raw edges of your quilt. Becau its stretchiness, bias binding works well for binding projects with curves or rounded corners and tends to smooth and flat in any given circumstance. It is also more durable than other types of binding.

MAKING CONTINUOUS BIAS STRIP BINDING

Bias strips for binding can simply be cut and pieced the desired length. However, when a long length of binding is needed, the "continuous" method is quick accurate.

1. Cut a square from binding fabric the size indica in the project instructions. Cut square in half diagonally to make 2 triangles.
2. With right sides together and using a $^1/_4$" seam allowance, sew triangles together (**Fig. 15**); pres seam allowance open.
3. On wrong side of fabric, draw lines the width of the binding as specified in the project instructions, usually $2^1/_2$" (**Fig. 16**). Cut off any remaining fabric less than this width.
4. With right sides inside, bring short edges togeth to form a tube; match raw edges so that first dra line of top section meets second drawn line of bottom section (**Fig. 17**).
5. Carefully pin edges together by inserting pins through drawn lines at the point where drawn lir intersect, making sure the pins go through intersections on both sides. Using a $^1/_4$" seam allowance, sew edges together. Press seam allowance open.
6. To cut continuous strip, begin cutting along first drawn line (**Fig. 18**). Continue cutting along dra line around tube.
7. Trim ends of bias strip square.
8. Matching wrong sides and raw edges, press bia strip in half lengthwise to complete binding.

ATTACHING BINDING WITH MITERED CORNERS

1. Beginning with one end near center on bottom edge of quilt, lay binding around quilt to make sure that seams in binding will not end up at a corner. Adjust placement if necessary. Matching raw edges of binding to raw edge of quilt top, pin binding to right side of quilt along one edge.

2. When you reach the first corner, mark ¼" from corner of quilt top (**Fig. 19**).

3. Beginning approximately 10" from end of binding and using a ¼" seam allowance, sew binding to quilt, backstitching at beginning of stitching and at mark (**Fig. 20**). Lift needle out of fabric and clip thread.

4. Fold binding as shown in **Figs. 21 – 22** and pin binding to adjacent side, matching raw edges. When you reach the next corner, mark ¼" from edge of quilt top.

5. Backstitching at edge of quilt top, sew pinned binding to quilt (**Fig. 23**); backstitch when you reach the next mark. Lift needle out of fabric and clip thread.

6. Continue sewing binding to quilt, stopping approximately 10" from starting point (**Fig. 24**).

Fig. 19

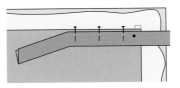

Fig. 20

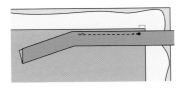

Fig. 21

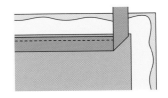

Fig. 22

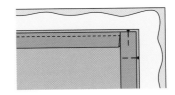

Fig. 23

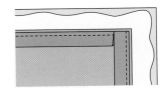

Fig. 24

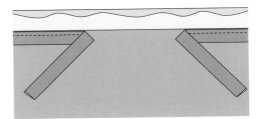

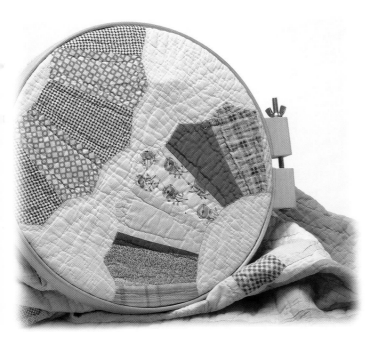

Fig. 25

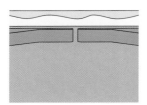

Fig. 26

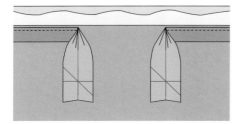

Fig. 27

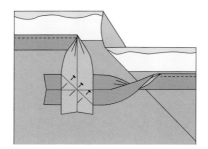

Fig. 28

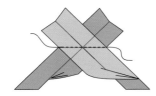

7. Bring beginning and end of binding to center of opening and fold each end back, leaving a $1/4$" space between folds (**Fig. 25**). Finger-press folds.

8. Unfold ends of binding and draw a line across wrong side in finger-pressed crease. Draw a line through the lengthwise pressed fold of binding at same spot to create a cross mark. With edge of ruler at marked cross, line up 45° angle marking on ruler with one long side of binding. Draw a diagonal line from edge to edge. Repeat on remaining end, making sure that the two lines are angled the same way (**Fig. 26**).

9. Matching right sides and diagonal lines, pin binding ends together at right angles (**Fig. 27**).

10. Machine stitch along diagonal line, removing pins as you stitch (**Fig. 28**).

11. Lay binding against quilt to double-check that it is correct length.

12. Trim binding ends, leaving $1/4$" seam allowance; press seam open. Stitch binding to quilt.

13. Trim backing and batting a scant $1/4$" larger than quilt top so that batting and backing will fill the binding when it is folded over to quilt backing.

14. On one edge of quilt, fold binding over to quilt backing and pin pressed edge in place, covering stitching line (**Fig. 29**). On adjacent side, fold binding over, forming a mitered corner (**Fig. 30**). Repeat to pin remainder of binding in place.

15. Blindstitch binding to backing, taking care not to stitch through to front of quilt. To blindstitch, come up at 1, go down at 2, and come up at 3 (**Fig. 31**). Length of stitches may be varied as desired.

Fig. 29

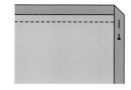

Fig. 30

Fig. 31

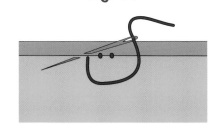

Metric Conversion Chart	
Inches x 2.54 = centimeters (cm)	Yards x .9144 = meters (m)
Inches x 25.4 = millimeters (mm)	Yards x 91.44 = centimeters (cm)
Inches x .0254 = meters (m)	Centimeters x .3937 = inches (")
	Meters x 1.0936 = yards (yd)

Standard Equivalents					
⅛"	3.2 mm	0.32 cm	⅛ yard	11.43 cm	0.11 m
¼"	6.35 mm	0.635 cm	¼ yard	22.86 cm	0.23 m
⅜"	9.5 mm	0.95 cm	⅜ yard	34.29 cm	0.34 m
½"	12.7 mm	1.27 cm	½ yard	45.72 cm	0.46 m
⅝"	15.9 mm	1.59 cm	⅝ yard	57.15 cm	0.57 m
¾"	19.1 mm	1.91 cm	¾ yard	68.58 cm	0.69 m
⅞"	22.2 mm	2.22 cm	⅞ yard	80 cm	0.8 m
1"	25.4 mm	2.54 cm	1 yard	91.44 cm	0.91 m

Production Team:

Technical Editor – Lisa Lancaster
Technical Writer – Frances Huddleston
Editorial Writer – Susan McManus Johnson
Graphic Artist – Dayle Carozza
Photography Stylist – Cassie Francioni
Staff Designers – Jean Lewis, Lisa Lancaster,
   and Frances Huddleston.

Endless Chain
was pieced by Nelwyn Gray,
quilted by Julie Schrader, and
bound by Diane Fischer.

Chinese Coins
was pieced by Lisa Lancaster,
quilted by Julie Schrader, and
bound by Diane Fischer.

Patriotic Sampler
was pieced by Larcie Burnett
and Nelwyn Gray.

Many thanks go to the
ladies for their beautiful wo